IMAGES
of America

FORT LEE

BIRTHPLACE OF THE
MOTION PICTURE INDUSTRY

The Fort Lee Film Commission (FLFC) was formed in 2000 by ordinance of the Mayor and Council of Fort Lee, New Jersey. The role of the film commission is to preserve films made in Fort Lee, to promote Fort Lee as a location for current filmmakers, and to educate through film retrospectives about Fort Lee's role as birthplace of the American film industry. The FLFC logo, pictured above, is a production still from *House of Hate* (Pathé, 1918) featuring movie serial queen Pearl White atop the Palisades. The FLFC has worked with the Fort Lee Public Library and its director, film scholar Rita Altamora, to digitize the library's collection of over 1,000 stills of Fort Lee–related film and studio history. The FLFC sponsors acquisitions of archival material for the Fort Lee Museum through donations. It provided assistance to member, film historian, and Rutgers University professor Richard Koszarski with his 2004 book *Fort Lee: The Film Town.*

On the cover: Actress Marion Davies appears, enjoying the music on the set of *The Dark Star* (Cosmopolitan-Paramount-Artcraft, 1919). Allan Dwan holds the megaphone while directing. (Fort Lee Film Commission.)

IMAGES
of America

FORT LEE
BIRTHPLACE OF THE
MOTION PICTURE INDUSTRY

Fort Lee Film Commission

ARCADIA
PUBLISHING

Published by Arcadia Publishing
Charleston SC, Chicago IL, Portsmouth NH, San Francisco CA

Printed in the United States of America

Library of Congress Catalog Card Number: 2006921282

For all general information contact Arcadia Publishing at:
Telephone 843-853-2070
Fax 843-853-0044
E-mail sales@arcadiapublishing.com
For customer service and orders:
Toll-Free 1-888-313-2665

Visit us on the Internet at www.arcadiapublishing.com

Most importantly, this book is a celebration of the work of local film historian Tom Hanlon. Hanlon produced *Before Hollywood There Was Fort Lee* in 1964. He screened this film and other Fort Lee silent films at the Fort Lee Public Library throughout the 1970s, and, as children in his audience, we would grow up to carry on his work through the formation of the Fort Lee Film Commission. If this book is dedicated to anyone it is to the memory of Tom Hanlon.

CONTENTS

ACKNOWLEDGMENTS

The Fort Lee Film Commission thanks Fort Lee mayor Jack Alter and members of the borough council and the people of Fort Lee, past and present, for their support and inspiration. This book and the success of the Fort Lee Film Commission in general would not be possible without the work of a corps of volunteers—Lou Azzollini, Kevin Ceragno, Ben Chirls, Stacy D'Arc, Aya Hamada, Patrick Hammer, Arya-Francesca Jenkins, Christina Kotlar, Cindy Mamary, and Scott Manginelli.

Special thanks go to the Fort Lee Historical Society and its president Robert Boylan and Fort Lee Library director Rita Altomara for the use of archival photographs from their collections. Thanks to Marc Wanamaker for stills from his collection at the Bison Archive, Patrick Loughney of the Library of Congress for images of *The Curtain Pole*, Pierre Courtet-Cohl, Anthony Slide, Joe Yranski, Joseph J. Licata, and Bluepoint Graphics. The Fort Lee Film Commission wishes to thank film historian David Shepard for his friendship and support and for his work on the restoration of the documentary *Before Hollywood There Was Fort Lee*. Thanks also go to Paul C. Spehr for his groundbreaking book *The Movies Begin: Making Movies in New Jersey 1887–1920*, which is a wonderful source of information on this period. Thanks to Richard Koszarski for his seminal book *Fort Lee: The Film Town* that is the first book dedicated to Fort Lee's role as birthplace of the American film industry.

INTRODUCTION

At the start of the 20th century, Fort Lee's place in American history was firmly identified with the role it had played in the American Revolution. Tales of George Washington and Tom Paine were part of local legend, and the most common historic artifacts to be found were cannon balls and cavalry swords. But as soon as Thomas Edison's first motion pictures began appearing on theater screens across the country, these founding fathers were joined by newcomers with names like Pickford, Griffith, and Sennett, and Fort Lee found itself making a new kind of history—film history.

Early moviemakers were attracted to the borough's scenic wonders—not just the historic Palisades, but an entire menu of forests, fields, farms, and waterfalls, all relatively unspoiled and within easy commuting distance of New York. Production crews from the Biograph and Edison Companies crossed the Hudson River each morning on the Fort Lee ferries, and the borough soon became so popular that rival studios began to compete for time at the most photogenic front porches or rock formations. The romance of this daily commute soon earned a special place in early motion picture lore.

Then in 1910, Mark Dintenfass (later a New Jersey gubernatorial candidate on the "Single Tax" platform) built the Champion studio at the end of Fifth Street in the Coytesville section of Fort Lee. Within months, great greenhouse studios began sprouting up all over the Fort Lee area. The Fort Lee studios transformed into crucial centers of production in an era when feature-length films replaced the old two-reelers, picture palaces supplanted nickelodeons and the motion picture star system was born.

By 1915, most American films were already being made in California, where land and labor were much cheaper. But the home offices in New York liked the idea of keeping some studios within commuting distance. Fort Lee filmmaking continued to flourish until a series of calamities struck in 1918: a wartime fuel shortage was followed by the coldest winter in memory, and no sooner was peace declared than a deadly influenza epidemic closed all the studios for weeks. Producers settled down in sunny California and never returned, and Fort Lee's studio facilities changed from production centers to storage and distribution facilities.

This book is not a chronological history of the movies in Fort Lee, but a snapshot of one New Jersey town whose history was changed forever by its brief encounter with a fabulous new industry. George Washington and his troops came and went within a few months in 1776, but the impact they left behind resonated for centuries. The movie studios flourished for a decade before moving on to sunnier climes. But, like Washington's army, they too, impacted the area and left a lasting legacy. To learn more about Fort Lee and its film history, readers may refer to *Hollywood on the Palisades* by Rita Altomara, the Fort Lee Historical Society's *Fort Lee, Fort Lee: The Film Town* by Richard Koszarski, and the Fort Lee Film Commission Web site www. fortleefilm.org.

Fort Lee Film Commission Members:
Tom Meyers—Executive Director
Nelson Page—Chairman
Kay Nest—Vice-Chair
Donna Brennan—Secretary
Richard Koszarski
Marc Perez
Councilman Armand Pohan—Liaison

These studio logos include many that are long forgotten. The Fox Film Company did not employ its still current 20th Century Fox logo until its merger with 20th Century in 1935. However, the Universal logo displayed here is the earliest example of a studio logo still in use today. The Biograph logo can be seen in the early Biograph films as it was displayed on the sets and thus captured on film as a method to prevent other companies from stealing Biograph footage.

One

THE STUDIOS

The world's first motion picture studio was a tar paper photographic shack built by Thomas Edison in West Orange; but within a few years, Edison, and the competing Biograph and Vitagraph companies, were placing rival stages atop Manhattan office buildings. Interior sets were built there to take advantage of natural light, while exteriors were shot on the streets, in public parks, or anywhere else within easy commuting distance. Most producers preferred to work in daylight and began to build large, greenhouse-style studios for themselves in the suburbs.

Fort Lee was discovered as a filming location by 1898 and soon became a favorite spot for unlicensed independent producers who were dodging detectives hired by Thomas Edison. One of these independents, Champion, built the first permanent studio in the Fort Lee area in 1910. By 1918, at least 11 major studios were operating on this side of the Hudson River.

These factories usually included a glass-enclosed shooting stage for film production and a laboratory for developing negatives and producing the positive prints that became films. Although studio activity drew the most attention, Fort Lee's role as a film lab and distribution center lasted far longer, and involved the community by employing local residents.

No one can say exactly how many films were made in and around Fort Lee during the early days of the motion picture industry, as few companies kept records of their location work. Legend has it that D. W. Griffith shot *The Birth of a Nation* in Fort Lee. What he actually made were three earlier Civil War pictures and probably a hundred or more short films and the exterior scenes for pictures like *The New York Hat*.

By 1914, feature length pictures had come to dominate the market and large new studios were constructed in Fort Lee to make use of New York theatrical talent uninterested in traveling to California just to make a movie. During the golden age of Fort Lee filmmaking, Fox, Paramount, Goldwyn and Universal all took advantage of the borough's proximity to Broadway to make many of their early features.

Film pioneer and studio executive Mark Dintenfass founded the Champion Film Company in 1910. The Champion studio built in the Coytesville section of Fort Lee was the first studio built in the Fort Lee area. In 1912, Dintenfass became an executive in the new Universal Film Manufacturing Company, founded by Carl Laemmle, and the Champion studio became part of Universal. Representative films of the Champion studio include the studio's first production *Abernathy Kids to the Rescue* (1910).

The Champion studio, pictured here, remains standing today on the dead end of Fifth Street. This building, used as a printing plant for decades, is the oldest standing studio structure in the nation. The Fort Lee Film Commission (FLFC) leads jitney tours of the historic film sites in the borough twice a year in the hope of creating greater awareness of the history of such structures as the Champion studio and of ensuring their permanent preservation.

Ideal Studios was opened in June 1916 in Hudson Heights atop the Palisades south of Fort Lee in present day Guttenberg by producer-director Herbert Brenon. The studio consisted of two buildings that were later converted for sound and used in such films as *The Golf Specialist* (1930), W. C. Fields' first talkie, produced by Radio Pictures.

In the film industry, Carl A. Willatowski was known as "Doc Willat," due to his degree in veterinary medicine. In October 1913, the Willat Manufacturing Company purchased property on the corner of Main Street and Linwood Avenue near the Éclair studio on Linwood Avenue. Willat built a modern film laboratory and two vaulted greenhouse studios there.

On June 8, 1912, Carl Laemmle joined forces with other independent filmmakers to form the Universal Film Manufacturing Company. On August 5, 1914, Laemmle purchased the land for an East Coast studio on Main Street in Fort Lee. For a short time, this studio was the largest in the country. Pictured are Laemmle (the shorter man) and Robert H. Cochrane at the groundbreaking for Universal's Fort Lee studio in 1914.

This is the Universal studio on Main Street, as it is being constructed in 1915. This would become the most famous and largest of all the studios in Fort Lee.

This is an aerial view of Universal studio property on Main Street. The administration building in the foreground was constructed and used by Consolidated/Republic Pictures. Republic Pictures chief Herbert J. Yates maintained an East Coast office in this building. This facility was one of the largest in terms of employment of Fort Lee residents. Consolidated operated out of this site from 1930 through 1961.

Pictured is an interior photograph of the Universal studio on Main Street, as actors and crews are posed for a photograph. Universal would shortly depart this facility for the newly built Universal City in California and Samuel Goldwyn would lease the Fort Lee studio. This studio was one of the most modern and the largest in the world at that time.

Universal Movie Studio. - Fort Lee N. J.

This postcard captures the image of Universal studio, as viewed from Main Street in the West Fort Lee section of town. The building was razed in 1963 and film storage facilities were expanded by Bonded. In 2006, the FLFC dedicated a historic marker on this site and will incorporate the location in a historic walking-tour map of the studio sites that will be produced in 2006.

This view of Universal captures the massive size of the buildings and the large water tower in the background. Universal founder Carl Laemmle originally envisioned this facility as Universal City East. Although Fort Lee lost Universal to Universal City in California, where the studio flourishes today, Fort Lee can lay claim to being the location of the first production of Universal founder Laemmle, and so, the start of Universal.

William Fox was a successful theater owner who started movie production in 1914 in the leased Willat studio in Fort Lee. This first home to Fox studio was the location where actress Theda Bara became a star in *A Fool There Was* (Fox Film Corporation, 1915). This was Fox's first big hit, which was followed by others starring Bara. The Willat studio was Fox's principal studio through 1920.

Pictured here are the managers of Fox Film Corporation at the Fort Lee studio, around July 3, 1915. Notice the extravagant set they appeared on for this photograph. The movie business, a few short years prior to this photograph, relied on nickelodeons. At the time of this photograph, the business had grown into an industry and picture palaces were being constructed to display the films of the studios.

This photograph depicts construction of a set on the Fox back lot in Fort Lee. Set design was an art form that flourished on the back lots of the Fort Lee Studios. Studios employed skilled carpenters and worked at a breakneck pace to keep up with the steady production schedule.

Here is a wide shot of Main Street looking west. The Fox studio (Willat) appears as the large structure to the right on the corner of Linwood Avenue. The trolley was a means of transportation for many of the studio crews (see tracks in foreground). The trolley also made appearances in numerous films when it was used in street scenes. The trolley stops were named after the studios.

This Los Angeles-based company leased production facilities at the Willat studios in 1915 and renamed the site the Triangle Film Corporation Fort Lee Studios and Laboratories. Keystone Films and Fine Arts Productions produced films at this facility for Triangle. Pictured here is Triangle at the time of Roscoe "Fatty" Arbuckle's residence at the studio, 1915–1916. The trees in the middle of Linwood Avenue hide the location of other studios.

Pictured on the back lot of the Willat studio are film industry pioneers, from left to right, E. J. Mock, C. O. Baumann, Thomas H. Ince, Mack Sennett, Charles Kessel, Irvin Willat, George Blaisdell, J. V. Ritchie, H. A. Palmer, William Johnston, Worthy Butts, E. J. McGovern, Doc Willat, Harry Ennis, Fred Beecroft, Wen Milligan, and Adam Kessel Jr. The buildings behind the water tower are part of Éclair Laboratory and Studio.

Goldwyn Pictures Corporation was formed in 1916 by Samuel Goldfish, Edgar and Archibald Selwyn. The name Goldwyn was formed through the combination of the names Goldfish and Selwyn. Goldfish became the dominant partner and later changed his name to Goldwyn. Goldwyn's first studio was in rented space at the Solax Studios on Lemoine Avenue. Goldwyn later rented space at the larger Universal studio on Main Street in 1917. Goldwyn's first film was *Polly of the Circus* (1917). Will Rogers made his first film, *Laughing Bill Hyde* (Goldwyn Pictures Corporation, 1918), at the Goldwyn studio in Fort Lee. Sam Goldwyn remained with this company until 1920, when he resigned in an ownership struggle with the studio in Hollywood. That studio was soon to be merged and become Metro-Goldwyn-Mayer (MGM). Samuel Goldwyn went into independent film production, and for the next 35 years produced some of the finest films of the 20th century, including *The Best Years of Our Lives* (Samuel Goldwyn Company, 1946). Goldwyn died at age 91 in 1974.

Pathé, which had a large studio of its own in Jersey City, leased the Solax studio for almost a year and produced many of its "Astra" titles here, including *The Naulahka* (Pathé-Astra, 1918). Arthur Miller photographed the film, which featured Doraldina, the first performer to be billed as an "exotic dancer."

Actor E. K. Lincoln built his studio in Grantwood, New Jersey, on what is now 735 Bergen Boulevard in 1915. In 1916–1917, Fox rented the studio. This studio was rented by numerous production companies throughout the 1920s, and thereafter, used for its lab facilities, until independent filmmaker Bud Pollard took over the studio in 1933, two years after it was outfitted for sound. In February 1932, it was announced that silent film comedian Harry Langdon would make a series of two-reelers at the studio. Unfortunately the Langdon film that was shot was never released and it disappeared.

Film industry pioneer Jules Brulatour incorporated Paragon on March 31, 1915. The studio was built on John Street in the western section of Fort Lee. Film director Maurice Tourneur was the creative partner of the organization. One of the original parts of the studio still stands on John Street. This view of Paragon was taken as the studio construction nears completion.

This is a wide shot view of the Paragon studio, as seen from John Street. This property and the remaining studio buildings were used by the Fort Lee Post Office through the 1970s.

Pictured is the last remaining structure of Paragon. This building still stands on John Street, adjacent to a townhouse complex. The FLFC is at work on a project to place historic markers on this film site, among others.

Lewis Selznick, father of David O. Selznick, left World Pictures in 1916 and formed his own production company. He leased the Solax studio in Fort Lee. The company name was changed to Select Pictures in 1917, when 50 percent of the company stock was purchased by Famous Players Pictures' president Adolph Zukor. Selznick gained control of the two companies and merged them into Selznick-Select in 1919. Selznick controlled most of the studio space in Fort Lee by 1920.

This photograph depicts simultaneous productions at Selznick studio in Fort Lee in 1920. Note all the extras in the background—these are Fort Lee residents being used as extras.

The French Éclair company opened an American branch in Fort Lee in 1911. The studio was built on Linwood Avenue (the present day site of Constitution Park). The facility included a modern film laboratory. In 1914, the first major film fire in Fort Lee destroyed the Éclair laboratory. Fox later used the Éclair studio, in addition to Willat, until 1920. Pictured here is the interior of the studio. In the center of this photograph, famed cameraman Francis Doublier can be seen setting up a camera for a scene.

Seen here is the exterior of Éclair studio on Linwood Avenue around 1913. This location would eventually encompass numerous studios, including Fox-Willat. The Éclair studio became the location for Constitution Park. The FLFC presents their annual summer-long "Movies and Music Under the Stars" program at this site.

The Éclair Film Company in Fort Lee is pictured here around 1912, prior to a western location trip.

In 1914, Lewis Selznick, following his short period with Universal, formed a new production company, Equitable Pictures. Equitable joined with a company founded by the Shubert Theatrical Company and Jules Brulatour's Peerless Pictures to form World Pictures. Production was centered at the Peerless studio, built in 1914 by Brulatour, adjacent to Éclair on Linwood Avenue. Pictured here on the set of *Love in a Hurry* (World Film Corporation, 1919), is actor Carlyle Blackwell at the center of attention. He is the man with dark hair who is looking down near the camera.

World studio carpenters building the interior of a house. The glass ceiling above made it possible for work to be done during the day without the aid of gas-powered heat because of the sunlight.

Preparing the set for *The Black Panther's Cub* (Ziegfeld Cinema Corporation, 1921), carpenters and electricians work in the spacious building. Three or four sets could be built at the same time.

This photograph of the set during production of *Vengeance* (World Film Corporation, 1918) is a great example of the production of film. The movie industry employed numerous extras, mostly locals from town.

Pictured here are construction workers building a railing for a production. In the background, boards have been painted of city buildings to create the illusion of the setting of a town.

Hundreds of Fort Lee residents gained employment at the studios—from dollar a day extras to stagehands, carpenters, film cutters, and laboratory workers. Pictured on this set are World studio workers. Note the sign atop the prop table on the set that reads, "Henderson." Dell Henderson, a World director, later went on to have a long career in Hollywood as an actor appearing in such films as *Men In Black* (Columbia, 1934), *It's A Gift* (Paramount, 1934), and *Abbott & Costello in Hollywood* (MGM, 1945).

Pictured here is the World studio crew on set between takes. Fort Lee studios employed large crews, who designed and constructed numerous sets on a daily basis. Crews, such as the one pictured here, started some of the first theatrical unions, such as the International Alliance of Theatrical Stage Employees (IATSE).

Alice Guy Blaché, the first woman director in cinema history, left Gaumont with her husband Herbert Blaché in 1910. They struck out on their own and formed the Solax Company. The Blachés opened production facilities for their new company in Flushing, New York, but within two years, they were so successful, they built a $100,000 studio facility in Fort Lee. Solax had its own film processing laboratory and state-of-the-art stages in Fort Lee. She later divorced and returned to France in 1922, never to make another film. Alice Guy Blaché returned to the United States in 1964 and died while living near the site of her old Solax studio in New Jersey in 1968.

The Solax studio is under construction on Lemoine Avenue in Fort Lee around 1912, Alice Guy Blaché appears in the foreground. The FLFC dedicated a historical marker at this site. It remains the only marker honoring her for the role she played in cinema history.

Metro Pictures was started in 1916, primarily as a distributor for Solax films. Several young stars appeared in these films, including John and Ethel Barrymore and Olga Petrova. Metro later became MGM. Pictured here are Ethel Barrymore and Charles Sutton in a still from *The Eternal Mother* (Metro Pictures, 1917).

Artcraft Pictures Corporation was formed as a prestigious offshoot of Famous Players–Lasky Corporation. Artcraft pictures were made in Famous Players' Hollywood and New York studios and the Paragon studio in Fort Lee. Pictured here in the production of *Pride of the Clan* (Artcraft Pictures Corporation, 1917) is the star of the film, Mary Pickford.

Kalem was formed in 1907 and its first productions were made in New York City. Kalem built an open-air studio in Cliffside Park near the Fort Lee border in 1913 at 199 Palisade Avenue. By 1915, Kalem had built a proper studio, but continued to maintain other studios outside of New Jersey. Among Kalem's best films are *The Vampire* (1913) and *Cabaret Dancer* (1914).

This still was captured from a slide from *Rescued from an Eagle's Nest* (Edison Company, 1907), the first film to feature D. W. Griffith as an actor. The film's director was J. Searle Dawley and the cameraman was Edwin S. Porter. *Rescued from an Eagle's Nest* was shot atop the Palisades in Fort Lee as well as in Edison's studio in the Bronx for process shots.

This version of *Little Red Riding Hood* was made in 1921 by Prizma Color, one of the first successful color film processes. George Ali, in costume as the wolf, was famous on stage and screen for his animal impersonations (he played "Nana" in Herbert Brenon's silent film version of *Peter Pan*). In his diaries, Fort Lee resident Jack Van Epps claims to have directed the film.

Two

THE FILMS

The streets of Fort Lee echo with the ghosts of Theda Bara, Roscoe "Fatty" Arbuckle, Mack Sennett, Mabel Normand, D. W. Griffith, and other film luminaries. D. W. Griffith first came to Fort Lee as an actor in the film, *Rescued from an Eagle's Nest.* In 1908, he returned as a director for Biograph and shot hundreds of films in Fort Lee between 1908 and 1912. While working in Fort Lee, Griffith and cameraman Billy Bitzer made innovations in editing, lighting, and cinematography. Griffith led others to the area and helped to transform Fort Lee into the first American film town.

Slapstick comedy traces its roots to *The Curtain Pole* (Biograph, 1909), which was filmed in Fort Lee. This D. W. Griffith film starred Mack Sennett and provided him with the first opportunity to express his style of comedy on film. Comedic greats, such as Roscoe "Fatty" Arbuckle and Mabel Normand followed Sennett to Fort Lee. The films made at Triangle studio in Fort Lee still bring laughter to audiences, as was proven at the 2006 Arbuckle film retrospective at the Museum of Modern Art in New York.

The exteriors of Carl Laemmle's first film *Hiawatha* (IMP, 1909) were shot in the Coytesville section of Fort Lee. Three years later, while still working in Fort Lee, Laemmle formed Universal. Laemmle gained control of the Champion studio in Fort Lee and, in 1914, built Universal studio on Main Street.

William Fox leased studio space at the Willat studio on Main Street and Linwood Avenue. This became the birthplace of what we know today as 20th Century Fox. The first star to emerge out of the Fox studio in Fort Lee was screen vamp Theda Bara. *A Fool There Was* (Fox Film Corporation, 1915) not only made Theda Bara the first sex symbol of the silver screen, but established Fox as a major studio.

These Fort Lee films represent a slice of the activity during the town's golden age of cinema, which also included independent films, African American films, Yiddish films, the first Mormon talkie *Corianton* (1931), and Italian American films made in the period from 1920 to 1948.

Éclair's *Robin Hood* was restored by the FLFC in 2006. FLFC member, film historian Richard Koszarski worked with the preservation team of Marc Perez, Kris Fraga, and John Sikes of Sirk Productions in New York City and with Metropolis Film Lab of New York City to complete this project.

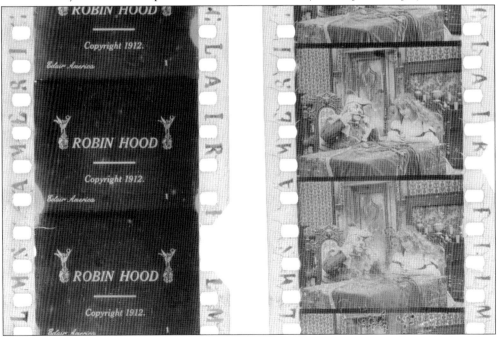

This is a surviving element from the original 35-millimeter silver nitrate film of *Robin Hood* (Éclair, 1912). Several elements from the original nitrate film were used by the FLFC in the restoration process. The bulk of the restoration was from a 16-millimeter source.

Shot at the Fox Studios in Fort Lee in 1915, this Theda Bara vehicle was directed by Raoul Walsh. Walsh's film beat West Coast–based director Cecil B. DeMille's production of the same name, *Carmen,* into theaters, providing studio owner William Fox with another hit film. Pictured in the production stills are Theda Bara, posing at a rock on the Fox back lot—note the roof line of Main Street structures in the background. Those buildings, along with the "Theda Bara Rock," are still visible at this Main Street location. The rock, once part of the Fox back lot, is situated in the courtyard of a garden apartment complex.

This still from *Sin* (Fox Film Corporation, 1915) gives a clue as to why it was banned in Ohio and Georgia—and also as to why it was another enormous hit for Fox. Theda Bara portrays an Italian peasant girl who travels to New York to follow her lover, a mobster. Her costar was Warner Oland, who would go on to screen fame for his portrayal of Charlie Chan.

The Darling of Paris (Fox Film Corporation, 1917) was another hit, Bara's fifth moneymaker in a row for Fox. This film was loosely based on Victor Hugo's *The Hunchback of Notre Dame*, but curiously, this film version features a hunchback who is cured. Theda Bara portrays the gypsy-dancing girl Esmeralda. The production still highlights the elaborate back-lot set constructed for the picture. The expensive sets were built in Fort Lee, and the reproduction of Notre Dame Cathedral was well received.

Adapted from the 1848 novel and 1852 play *La Dame aux Camellias* by Alexandre Dumas, *Camille* (Fox Film Corporation, 1917) was a modern day version of the doomed French courtesan's life, portrayed by Theda Bara.

This Theda Bara vehicle, *Heart and Soul* (Fox Film Corporation, 1917), was adapted from the 1887 novel *Jess* by H. Rider Haggard. The plot involves a Hawaiian maiden who sacrifices herself for the happiness of her sister.

Mary Pickford, seated at desk, starred in this silent comedy drama *The Poor Little Rich Girl* (Artcraft Pictures, 1917) directed by Maurice Tourneur. Pickford plays lonely and unhappy Gwendolyn, whose rich parents ignore her and whose servants push her around. This film was selected to the National Film Registry, Library of Congress, in 1991.

Mary Pickford pictured here with her director Maurice Tourneur on the set of *The Poor Little Rich Girl* at the Paragon studio on John Street. Tourneur was one of the greatest directors to work in Fort Lee. His surviving films, such as *The Wishing Ring* (World Film Corporation, 1914) and *The Blue Bird* (Famous Players–Lasky Corporation, 1918), are among the best ever shot here.

Hiawatha (IMP, 1909) was the first film produced by Carl Laemmle, later the founder of Universal. The film was made for Laemmle's Independent Motion Picture Company of America (IMP). Most of the location work was done in the Coytesville section of Fort Lee.

This frame grab from the D. W. Griffith–directed short *The Lonely Villa* (Biograph, 1909) shows Bigler Street in the foreground and Hudson Terrace in the background, the area of the present day approach to the George Washington Bridge. The film was important because Griffith employed cross-cutting to build excitement. It also represents one of Mary Pickford's early screen appearances.

Robert Warwick and Stella Archer starred in *The Face in the Moonlight* (World Pictures, 1915), a silent costume drama taken from a play by Charles Osborne. Frenchman Albert Capellani directed this film.

Here is actress Claire Whitney being courted in *East Lynne* (Fox Film Corporation, 1916), which also starred Theda Bara. In the film, Bara, everyone's favorite vamp, is miscast as a long-suffering lady in a modern setting. A print of this film was acquired from Fox by the Museum of Modern Art in 1971, making it one of the few Bara feature films to survive the silent era. Directed by Bertram Bracken, the story was adapted from a play by Mary Elizabeth Braddon.

Pictured here is a scene from *A Girl's Folly* (World Pictures, 1917), directed by Maurice Tourneur and shot at Paragon studio. Extras are captured walking down John Street to the studio. The plot of the film is a young woman from the country coming to the city to break into the movies. The Paragon is captured in full production in the film.

This independent feature, *The Pinch Hitter* (Oscar Price Productions, 1925), was shot at the Paragon studio on John Street. Directed by Joseph Henabery, the film starred Glenn Hunter (pictured here) and Fort Lee resident Constance Bennett in an early role. The silent comedy was adapted from an earlier film written by C. Gardner Sullivan.

GLENN HUNTER . "The PINCH HITTER" ... CONSTANCE BENNETT

The Fighting Blade (Inspiration Pictures, 1923), an early swashbuckler, featured Richard Barthelmess and Dorothy Mackaill. The director was John S. Robertson and Everett Shinn was art director. Barthelmess played against type in this romantic costume drama as he portrayed a swashbuckling soldier of fortune.

Hope Hampton's mentor, producer, and fiancé Jules Brulatour, provided her with every advantage in the drama *Stardust* (Hobart Henley Productions, Inc., 1922), including the option of James Rennie as her costar. Pictured here is Hampton with director Hobart Henley. The movie was based on a novel by Fanny Hurst.

This is a frame grab from the film *Symbol of the Unconquered* (Micheaux Film Corporation, 1920), showing actress Iris Hall walking on the corner of Second Street and Washington Avenue in the Coytesville section of Fort Lee. The film was shot in the same neighborhood as the Champion studio, which was probably used by Micheaux for interiors. A key segment of *Symbol of the Unconquered* dealt with the black community successfully repelling a raid by the Ku Klux Klan.

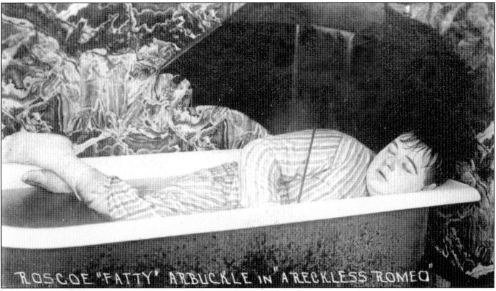

This formerly "lost" film, *A Reckless Romeo* (Comique Film Corporation, 1917), was discovered by the Norwegian Film Institute in 1999 and restored through joint efforts with the George Eastman House. Filmed at the Palisades Amusement Park and on Main Street near the intersection of Linwood Avenue, this two-reeler spotlights the talents of comedian Roscoe "Fatty" Arbuckle. Arbuckle played a philandering husband whose antics at Palisades Amusement Park were caught by a newsreel cameraman and displayed at the local movie house for an audience that included his wife and mother-in-law.

The Curtain Pole (Biograph, 1909) used the streets of Fort Lee to great advantage as a young Mack Sennett led one of the first slapstick chases in cinema history. Pictured is a scene filmed on Eichoff Street (now Gerome Avenue) with Main Street storefronts in the background. The poster-covered fence in the background ran between Ferrando's Flats (currently a jewelry store) and McNally Brothers Funeral Home on the right. Sennett appears holding the curtain pole in the foreground in this D. W. Griffith–directed film. Three years later Sennett formed his Keystone studio in Fort Lee.

This frame grab from *The Curtain Pole* shows Mack Sennett on the porch of a house on Main Street. Note the buildings of the Holy Angels Academy on the left hand side of the picture.

This short, *The Musketeers of Pig Alley* (Biograph, 1912), is often considered the first gangster film in history. Directed by D. W. Griffith and written by Griffith and Anita Loos, the film is also credited for its early use of follow-focus, a cinematic technique still in use today. The scene pictured here was shot on Main Street in Fort Lee. Lillian Gish is pictured in the foreground with eyes downcast.

The Cord of Life (Biograph, 1909) was shot in January 1909. Pictured in this frame grab are Mack Sennett and Charles Inslee crossing Main Street. Director D. W. Griffith used cutbacks in his film to increase the suspense as a father races home from work to thwart a criminal who is suspending his baby from a high window.

Barbary Sheep (Paramount-Artcraft, 1917) was shot at the Paragon studio on John Street. Directed by Maurice Tourneur, it featured extravagant exterior and interior sets, which made this section of Fort Lee look like Algeria. Costume designer Madame Borries provided the cast with authentic Far East attire. Pictured here is actress Elsie Ferguson filming a scene on the outdoor set.

Barbary Sheep took advantage of elaborate studio sets in the Paragon, such as the one pictured here with Elsie Ferguson. Again, these sets, combined with the authentic costumes, which satisfied filmgoers in 1917, proved that the studios of Fort Lee could rival Hollywood in set design.

The plot of *The Blue Bird* (Famous Players–Lasky Corporation, 1918) had the main characters, Mytyl (Tula Belle) and Tyltyl (Robin MacDougall) as two children searching for the blue bird of happiness. Director Maurice Tourneur employed fantastic special effects created by designer Benjamin Carre and reminiscent of George Melies. *The Blue Bird* was copied from a silver nitrate 35-millimeter print by the George Eastman House as part of the Saving America's Treasures Program of the National Endowment for the Arts and the Film Preservation Foundation.

This Fox studio production of *Les Miserables* (Fox Film Corporation, 1918) featured the largest outdoor set ever built in Fort Lee. *Les Miserables* has long been considered lost, but a copy has recently been found in Warsaw, Poland, by FLFC member Richard Koszarski; the FLFC is currently negotiating to have the film brought to the United States, so that it can undergo restoration.

Cliffhanger serial queen Pearl White reached the pinnacle of screen fame in *The Perils of Pauline* (Pathé, 1914), which was shot in and around Fort Lee. Among the locations used for this blockbuster movie serial were the cliffs of the Fort Lee Palisades and Palisades Amusement Park. Pictured here is Pearl in white near the stand with Crane Wilbur. This 1914 film is significant as it marked the screen debut of six-year-old Milton Berle, who, in his biography, claimed this as his first acting job.

The Perils of Pauline needed effective villains to create the "perils" for Pearl that would make moviegoers return each week to discover the outcome of every cliffhanger. Pictured here are actors Paul Panzer and Crane Wilbur. Wilbur played the hero who was always helping Pauline. Panzer was the evil secretary who pretended to help Pauline, but was always trying to get her killed.

The 15-chapter movie serial *The Black Secret* (Pathé, 1919) saw Pearl play a secret service agent who suspected her boss was being employed by the enemy. This was Pearl's ninth serial in five years. She subsequently left Pathé for Fox, where she made a series of melodramas that were less successful than her serials. Pearl moved to Paris, France, where she remained until her death in 1938. The queen of American movie serials is buried in the Passy Cemetery in Paris.

The Eternal Magdalene (Goldwyn Pictures Corporation, 1919) was likely shot at the Solax studio on Lemoine Avenue, which was leased by Samuel Goldwyn prior to the Universal on Main Street. Pictured here on the set is director Arthur Hopkins with actress Maxine Elliot. Phil Rosen was the cinematographer on this film. He started his career in the silent era and would go on to direct for studios such as Universal, Paramount, and MGM through 1949.

Exteriors for *The New York Hat* (Biograph, 1912) were shot on Main Street and in the Coytesville section of Fort Lee. This film starred Mary Pickford to great effect as the young woman who longs for the elusive New York Hat. Biograph stock company actor Lionel Barrymore appeared as the local minister. Anita Loos of *Gentleman Prefer Blondes* fame was one of the foremost screenwriters of the early cinema; this was her first produced screenplay. Pictured here is Mary Pickford outside St. Stephen's Church on Washington Avenue in a scene from the film.

Samuel Goldwyn hired Ziegfeld Follies star Will Rogers to make his screen debut in *Laughing Bill Hyde* (Goldwyn Pictures Corporation, 1918). Rogers filmed in Fort Lee for Goldwyn while he continued to appear in the Ziegfeld Follies on Broadway. This was the start of a spectacular screen career that carried Rogers to fame in talkies at Fox studio in Hollywood and only ended with his tragic death in a plane crash in 1935. Rogers employed a formula that worked, he basically played himself on screen in *Laughing Bill Hyde*.

Shot in the Universal studio on Main Street, *The Enchanted Cottage* (Inspiration Pictures, 1924) benefited from wonderful studio sets that set the mood of the picture. Starring Richard Barthelmess and Mae McAvoy, this delicate drama involved a battle-scarred World War I veteran and a homely spinster who appear beautiful to one another while living in this enchanted cottage. The film was remade in 1945 by RKO with Robert Young and Dorothy McGuire.

Pictured here in a still from *The Vampire* (Kalem Company, 1913) are Alice Eis and Bert French as they perform their "Vampire Dance" on the open-air stage of Kalem's studio, just south of Fort Lee on Palisade Avenue in Cliffside Park. Directed by Robert Vignola, *The Vampire* beat Fox's Theda Bara vehicle *A Fool There Was* (Fox Film Corporation, 1915) to the screen by over one year.

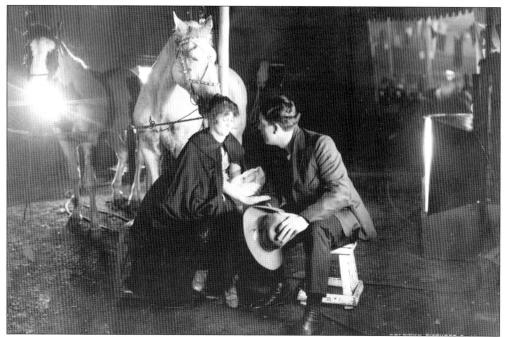

Polly of the Circus (Goldwyn Pictures Corporation, 1917) was the first release of the Goldwyn Pictures Corporation and was shot at the Universal studio in Fort Lee. Mae Marsh, pictured here, starred in the authentic circus drama.

The three-reel feature *Our Minister* (Kalem Company, 1913) was adapted from the drama by Denam Thompson and George W. Ryer. The film featured Kalem stars Alice Joyce and Tom Moore. Joyce, one of the great beauties of the silent cinema, was a telephone operator before she became a star for Vitagraph and Kalem.

Goldwyn was able to insert a World War I story line into a traditional mystery with a plot involving a top-secret mission to expose a nest of German spies in *The Face in the Dark* (Goldwyn Pictures Corporation, 1918). Goldwyn actress Mae Marsh played the daughter of a retired U.S. Secret Service agent. Pictured here is Mae Marsh in the bank safecracking scene.

The World War I propaganda film *The Prussian Cur* (Fox Film Corporation, 1918) was written and directed by Raoul Walsh and featured his wife, actress Miriam Cooper. Capt. Horst von der Goltz played the villain. In actuality, von der Goltz was a captured German spy who cooperated with the allies and was given asylum in the United States, where he found work in the movie industry.

DOROTHY GISH,

Born in Ohio in 1898, Dorothy Gish was already a veteran actress by the time she began working in silent films. Dorothy and Lillian Gish met director D. W. Griffith in 1912 and went to work for his Biograph stock company. Dorothy Gish was a talented light comedienne and pantomimist. Her final screen appearance was in Otto Preminger's *The Cardinal* (Columbia Pictures, 1963). She died in 1968 at age 70.

LILLIAN GISH

Lillian Gish, older sister of Dorothy, was born in 1893. Her first role was in a D. W. Griffith short, *An Unseen Enemy* (Biograph, 1912). Lillian went on to star in many of Griffith's most acclaimed films and became known as "The First Lady of the Silent Screen." She was the recipient of many awards. Her last film was *The Whales of August* in 1987. She died at age 99.

Three

PEOPLE AND PLACES

Fort Lee's memorable faces during the silent film era ran from the exotic; as with vamp Theda Bara, to that of the first woman director, Alice Guy Blaché. There were also the character-lined visages of local women who were able to secure employment at the studios as extras and film cutters. The employment of women at this time was a rarity, although the film industry in Fort Lee found a place for women in the days before they had acquired the right to vote. Generations of Fort Lee women, as well as men, were able to work in the movie industry in the film storage and lab facilities in Fort Lee throughout the 20th century. The film industry was new, although some doors that opened in Fort Lee would be closed when the industry moved west. The career of African American film pioneer Oscar Micheaux was a perfect example of this. Although he was able to produce films in Fort Lee through 1948, he was never able to work in Hollywood.

Among the local faces to enter the industry, the one that achieved the most success was Fort Lee–born Eddie Mannix. Mannix, born in the Coytesville section of Fort Lee in 1891, found his road to success with his employment at Palisades Amusement Park. Hired first as a bouncer by brothers Nicholas and Joseph Schenck, Eddie began handling the books for the Schenck's Palisades Amusement Park. The Schencks entered the movie industry shortly thereafter and Eddie managed the Comique Studios in New York City for Joseph Schenck. Through their association with Marcus Loew, the Schencks were involved in the founding of MGM and Mannix was sent by MGM president Nicholas Schenck to Hollywood, where he eventually became a trusted lieutenant to MGM chief Louis B. Mayer.

The people of Fort Lee became the backdrop of this burgeoning film town. Fort Lee, a small rural town atop the cliffs of the Palisades, was transformed overnight into a colony of studios that not only provided excitement, but employment. Locals rubbed elbows with the likes of Douglas Fairbanks, Mary Pickford, and Lon Chaney while they worked alongside them as colleagues.

Stage actor Maurice Barrymore (father of Ethel, John, and Lionel Barrymore) lived in this house at the beginning of the last century. Maurice staged a number of events to raise funds for the construction of a firehouse in the neighborhood and to purchase uniforms for the fire department volunteers. The Barrymore House (built in 1876) was demolished in 2002 to make way for development, despite the efforts of the FLFC and numerous citizens, including elementary school students of the nearby Public School No. 3.

Stage and screen star, the "Great Profile" John Barrymore (right) began his theatrical career in 1900 while living with his father in their Coytesville house. Then 18-year-old John Barrymore made his stage debut at a Fort Lee Fire Department fund-raiser, organized by his father Maurice. Lionel began his film career for Biograph in 1908, and he was a member of D. W. Griffith's Biograph stock company, which shot extensively in the neighborhood of the Barrymore House. The films Lionel appeared in with Fort Lee exteriors included *The New York Hat* (Biograph, 1912). Ethel Barrymore worked in Fort Lee for Metro Pictures. Ethel is pictured here in a still from the film *The Awakening of Helena Ritchie* (Metro Pictures Corporation, 1916). Notice the resemblance between Ethel Barrymore and Drew Barrymore—Ethel is Drew's great-aunt.

Monument Park was dedicated in 1908 in honor of the soldiers of the American Revolution stationed in Fort Lee from July through November 1776. The monument is visible in this photograph from *The Volunteer* (World Pictures, 1917), which starred child actress Madge Evans. It can be seen as early as 1909 in D. W. Griffith's *The Cord of Life* (Biograph).

The Fort Lee Theatre, built in 1919, was the second movie house in Fort Lee and the first to be constructed as a theater. This theater was later renamed the Metro, in honor of Fort Lee native and MGM executive, Eddie Mannix. This building still stands at 250 Main Street.

Ferrando's was by 1910 the first movie theater in Fort Lee and was converted from a schoolhouse. Today the Fort Lee Post Office parking lot on Main Street occupies the site.

Built near the George Washington Bridge on Lemoine Avenue in 1950, the Lee Theater offered a large balcony area. The Lee Theater operated until 1973, when it was demolished for proposed large-scale development of the downtown area. This spot remained undeveloped for 33 years. In 2006, construction began on new development that will include a four-screen independent cinema and attached film museum.

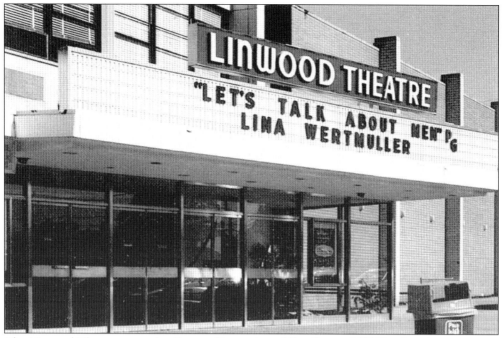

The Linwood Theatre, near the Coytesville section of Fort Lee at 1681 Fletcher Avenue, was a popular destination for moviegoers from the 1960s through the mid-1980s. Presently a CVS store occupies the building.

The Grant-Lee Theater was a fixture at 815 Abbott Boulevard in the Palisades section of Fort Lee. This movie-house was the last cinema in Fort Lee when it closed in the 1980s under the name Sharon Cinema. Today retail space occupies the building.

As a child, Nita Naldi attended the Academy of the Holy Angels situated on the corner of Main Street and Linwood Avenue in Fort Lee. Legend has it that Nita snuck out of class to climb over studio walls. She became a star in the John Barrymore film, *Dr. Jekyll and Mr. Hyde* (1920) and was dubbed the female Valentino. Nita Naldi died in 1961 at age 63.

Tallulah Bankhead, born in Huntsville, Alabama, in 1903, first appeared in the Goldwyn film *Thirty A Week* (1918) shot in Fort Lee. Bankhead went on to fame in such Hollywood classics as Alfred Hitchcock's *Life Boat* (20th Century Fox, 1944).

Action and adventure star Douglas Fairbanks made a number of films at the Triangle-Fine Arts studio in 1916 and the Paramount-Artcraft Studios in 1917. He is pictured here in a scene from the film *Wild and Woolly* (1917). Fairbanks later married another Fort Lee movie star, Mary Pickford.

Rambo's Hotel was a popular saloon during the silent movie era. D. W. Griffith used the location for exterior shoots and dressing rooms and for hiring movie extras, such as Milton Berle, who was selected as an extra during a cattle call at Rambo's while still a child. He appeared in his first film, *The Perils Of Pauline* (Pathé, 1914) in Fort Lee. The saloon closed in the early 1980s.

D. W. Griffith (right) is considered by many to be the supreme silent film artist. He was a legitimate stage actor for some years before his career as a filmmaker began. As an actor for the Edison Company, he appeared in *Rescued From An Eagle's Nest* (1907), shot in Fort Lee. He directed nearly 100 films in Fort Lee for Biograph Studios. Pictured with Griffith is his famed cameraman Billy Bitzer.

Roscoe "Fatty" Arbuckle rivaled Charlie Chaplin in popularity during the early days of the cinema. Fort Lee was critical to Arbuckle's growth as a filmmaker. Mack Sennett sent Arbuckle to Triangle Studios in Fort Lee in 1915–1916. In 2005, the FLFC curated a major film retrospective on Arbuckle. The Museum of Modern Art curated the most comprehensive Arbuckle film festival to date in the spring of 2006.

Mabel Normand, the first major American film comedienne, worked in Fort Lee with D. W. Griffith and Biograph. Her films here for Griffith include *Her Awakening* (1911) and *The Eternal Mother* (1911). She appeared in Mack Sennett's first Keystone Comedies (shot in Fort Lee in 1912) and later worked here again with Fatty Arbuckle (1916) and Goldwyn (1918).

Herbert Brenon moved into the Ideal studio in Hudson Heights in 1916, where he made such films as *The Fall of the Romanoffs*. He is shown here with his secretary, Miola De Pass. After leaving Fort Lee, Brenon directed many notable silent films, including *Peter Pan*, *Beau Geste*, and *The Great Gatsby*.

Barbara Tennant starred for American Éclair Studios in Fort Lee starting in 1911. Trained as a Shakespearean actress, she appeared in such Éclair films as *Robin Hood* (1912), *The Beaten Path* (1913), and *Firelight* (1914). Tennant signed with the World Film Corporation in 1915. Tennant is pictured here in a still from the World film *The Butterfly* (1915).

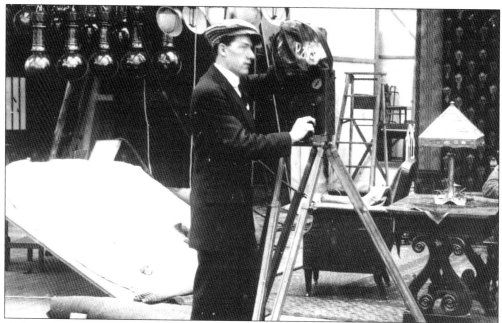

Arthur C. Miller began his career as a cinematographer while working with Fred Balshofer, founder of the early independent film company Bison, and became one of the industry's first newsreel cameramen while working for Pathé News. He later worked on Pathé's Pearl White serials. Pictured here is Miller at the Pathé studio in Jersey City.

Born in 1885 as Theodosia Goodman, Theda Bara was the prototype for the movie vamp. Bara's films for Fox Studios in Fort Lee include *Sin* (1915), *The Devil's Daughter* (1915), *Carmen* (1915), *The Serpent* (1916), *The Eternal Sappho* (1916), *Romeo and Juliet* (1916), and *Camille* (1917). Practically all of her films were destroyed in the July 9, 1937, fire at the Fox studio film storage facility in Little Ferry, New Jersey.

Joan Bennett was born in the Palisades section of Fort Lee. During her film career, she was under contract with Warner Brothers, Fox, and Paramount. Her leading men included Spencer Tracy, Ronald Colman, James Mason, Edward G. Robinson, and Humphrey Bogart. The Bennett house still stands at 1074 Dearborn Road in the Palisades section of Fort Lee.

This Constance Bennett still is from the Pathé film *Into the Net* (1924). Born in 1904, she was the first of the Bennett sisters to make her way into films. She made *The Pinch Hitter* (1925) at Paragon studio in Fort Lee. Constance was first under contract to Samuel Goldwyn and was featured in sophisticated comedies, such as *Topper* (1937), playing opposite Cary Grant. She died in 1966.

Madge Evans was a popular child actress for World Pictures in Fort Lee. Her films include *The Little Church Around The Corner* (1916), *The Devil's Toy* (1916), *The Burglar* (1917), *The Volunteer* (1917), *Wanted, A Mother* (1918), and *The Love Nest* (1919). She also worked for Fox Studios in such films as *True Blue* (1918), and for Famous Players Film Company. Evans did not migrate west until the 1930s. Her Hollywood films include *Pennies From Heaven* (Columbia, 1936) starring Bing Crosby.

Legendary queen of the movie serials, Pearl White is best known for her role in *The Perils of Pauline* (Pathé, 1914). She appeared in a number of serials shot atop Fort Lee's Palisades, which helped to establish the cliffhanger as a part of America's movie heritage. Upon its creation in 2000, the FLFC chose as its logo Pearl White atop the Palisades in a production still from *House of Hate*.

Best known for her relationship with newspaper tycoon William Randolph Hearst, Marion Davies was born Marion Douras in Brooklyn, New York, in 1897. She appeared onstage in a number of shows, including the Ziegfeld Follies. Hearst appeared in her life at this point and they formed Cosmopolitan Productions. Davies appeared in *The Dark Star* (Cosmopolitan-Paramount-Artcraft, 1919), shot at Paragon studio in Fort Lee.

The roots of American slapstick comedy can be directly traced to Mack Sennett's Fort Lee films, where Sennett started as an actor with the Biograph Company. He starred in *The Curtain Pole* (1909), one of the first slapstick comedies, directed by D. W. Griffith. Its chase sequence was shot in the Main Street area. Sennett formed his Keystone Company in Fort Lee in 1912.

Hope Hampton was discovered by film pioneer Jules Brulatour while working as an extra for director Maurice Tourneur. This Texas-born, Philadelphia beauty-contest winner made her screen debut in *A Modern Salome* (1920) and went on to star in several of Brulatour's financed films. Hampton starred in *The Unfair Sex* (Diamant Film Company, 1926), one of the last silent features shot in Fort Lee.

Francis Doublier's career began in 1894, when the 16 year old became associated with Lumière brothers and their experimentation with motion picture photography. From 1896 to 1900, Doublier went on tour, recording the first motion picture images of Europe, Asia, and Africa. He lived on 2011 Lemoine Avenue and eventually formed his own company, Palisade Film Laboratories, in the old E. K. Lincoln studio on Bergen Boulevard and documented local events in Fort Lee.

Fort Lee resident Jack Van Epps documented his work at the studios in his diary (pictured on this page). Van Epps, like other Fort Lee residents, found work at the studios and was a beneficiary of the economic boom brought to Fort Lee by the development of the motion picture industry. He later managed the Fort Lee Theatre on Main Street.

1915		
12/8		Fort Lee. NJ. Universal Studio. Worked as piano player in picture called "Autumn". Oscar Lund Director. Violet Mersereau, Star. Charlie Mundt secured job for me and May. She worked as a Dancer (Round). Both paid $5. Make-up, yellow grease and powder. Shaded cheeks for sunken appearance. Eyes and eyebrows lined.
		9-Worked same as yesterday in Western gambling house and dance hall.
	NY	May and I to Jim's for supper. NY. May took Jackie to Grandma's.
12/10		10-Worked at Universal again, same as yesterday. Sung songs for Lund. Cameraman took Close-up of me at Piano.
		May worked as 'Peasant' at Peerless Studio for "Brown, 'Turner', in The Genius" with George Beban. $5. She came up to me at Universal after she was through at Peerless. Jim's for supper. Then he and I down to Club. Pinochle. W. $6.
12/11		11-Peerless again. Miner in 'McTaigue'. Assist Bobby Graham told me smudge looked well in picture and introduced me to Genl Mgr. Us 5 miners out to old house and took scenes. Phoned May at Jim's she had better go home to NY.
12/13		13-Fort Lee but no work. Blizzard. Katherine's. Clothes drenched, May's feet wet. She caught cold.
		14-Powers to get Banknotes I was having printed. Pai $12. for them but they were not properly done.
12/14		Eve-Fort Lee Athletic Club Stag. Played, sang and talked for them.
		18-Saw Lou Tellegen in "The Unknown" at Broadway Theatre.
		Eve-Delaware Club. Saw Brady, Giebler, EddyShea (tim), Bender etal
12/20		20-Ft Lee. No work. May and I to Jim's overnight.
12/21		Ft Lee. Universal Studio. Worked extra as letter-carrier, Harry Myers.
12/23		Ray Blake and Madeline came to Scamper at Rats.
12/24		New York Theatre. Saw Vivian Martin in "Overnight". Then Rats
12/25		Xmas. Jackie got presents from Santa Claus. Ma's for dinner. Gifts velocipede for Jackie. Supper at Moore's. Jim and Katherine down from Ft Lee. Jim gave May and Jackie $2.50 gold pieces each.

Pictured here is an excerpt of Jack Van Epps diary of industry activities.

Alice Guy Blaché is pictured here on horseback in front of 2011 Lemoine Avenue, the house that Doublier bought from her in Fort Lee. Solax moved to Fort Lee in 1912. Blaché directed approximately 1,000 films; of these, about 100 survive. The films shot at the Solax studio number several hundred. In 2002, the FLFC dedicated a historic marker to Alice Guy Blaché at the former site of her Solax studio on Lemoine Avenue in Fort Lee. In 2006, the FLFC established the Alice Award to be given yearly to a Fort Lee High School student who shows the most promise in filmmaking courses.

"The Man of a Thousand Faces," Lon Chaney, starred in the film *The Light in the Dark* (Hope Hampton Productions, 1922). Jules Brulatour hired Clarence Brown to direct Chaney and actress Hope Hampton in this film. A restored print of this film was screened at the American Museum of the Moving Image during a November 2004 retrospective series on Fort Lee films. Chaney went on to his greatest fame when he starred in both *The Hunchback of Notre Dame* (1923) and *The Phantom of the Opera* (1925) for Universal.

Mary Pickford, dubbed America's sweetheart, was born in Canada in 1893. Broadway producer David Belasco was responsible for changing her name from Gladys Smith to Mary Pickford. Pickford made her screen debut as an extra in the Biograph short, directed by D. W. Griffith, *The Lonely Villa* (exteriors shot in Fort Lee). Her most famous Fort Lee film was *The New York Hat* (1912), her last film for Griffith and Biograph.

Born in Arlington, Massachusetts, in 1899, June Caprice won a Mary Pickford look-alike contest and was signed by William Fox. She chose her screen name from her first film, *Caprice of the Mountains* (1916). The opposite of fellow Fox star Theda Bara in her screen persona, June starred in Pickford-like films on the Fox lot in Fort Lee and enjoyed some success. Her last film was *The Sky Ranger* (1921).

The popular entertainer Irene Castle, part of the famous dance team of Vernon and Irene Castle, became a leading lady on the screen during World War I. Her husband, Vernon Castle, was killed in World War I. Irene starred in many Pathé films shot in Fort Lee in 1917–1918, including *Sylvia of the Secret Service* (1917) and *The Mark of Cain* (1917). She shot *The Firing Line* (1919) for Famous Players–Lasky Corporation at their studio in Fort Lee.

Born in Summit, New Jersey, in 1897, Marguerite Gabrielle Courtot began her career as an actress at the age of 15. Marguerite starred for Kalem at their Cliffside Park studio, just south of Fort Lee. She appeared in *The Vampire* (1913), *Uncle Tom's Cabin* (1913), and *The Girl and the Bachelor* (1914). Courtot left Kalem for Famous Players, Selznick, and Pathé, where she starred in the serials *Bound and Gagged* (1919) and *Pirate Gold* (1920).

Born in New York City in 1896, Muriel Henriette Ostriche (born Oestrich) started as an extra with the Biograph Studios in 1911. She was the Moxie Cola girl. With American Éclair in Fort Lee, she appeared in *Robin Hood* (1912). Ostriche was with Universal and Vitagraph, and later released films through Arrow Productions. She died in 1989 at the age of 93.

Virginia Pearson was a resident of Fort Lee, and lived on Cumbermeade Road. She appeared in Pathé's film *The Stain* (1914) with a new actress, Theda Bara, who would have a profound impact on her career. Pearson had starred in the original 1909 Broadway play *A Fool There Was*. Prior to her retirement in 1932, her most prominent film of the 1920s was Universal's *The Phantom of the Opera* (1925).

Born in Louisiana on April Fool's Day, 1902, Mary Miles Minter's real name was Juliet Reilly. She appeared onstage at the age of six. Her greatest stage success was in *The Littlest Rebel*. Minter entered films in 1915. She appeared in *Barbara Frietchie* (1915) for Metro Pictures Corporation in Fort Lee. Minter's career was cut short due to the scandal surrounding the unsolved murder of film director William Desmond Taylor in his Hollywood bungalow in 1922.

Ideal Studios opened in June 1916 and overlooked the Palisades. William Claude Dukenfield, better known as W. C. Fields, shot his first talking picture, *The Golf Specialist*, at Ideal in April 1930. The Marx Brothers preceded Fields at Ideal by starring here in their first film, *Humor Risk* (1921) (unreleased).

Emile Cohl, "The Father of the Animated Cartoon," came to Fort Lee from France in 1912 and is seen sitting second from right with Francis Doublier and his family at his house on Hoyt Street. While with Gaumont in France, Cohl created the first fully animated film *Fantasmagorie* (1908). Upon his arrival in Fort Lee, he began work with the American Éclair studio on Linwood Avenue.

This 16-year-old model and actress's involvement with New York City architect Stanford White resulted in the crime of the century when Evelyn Nesbit's then-husband, Harry K. Thaw, murdered White atop the Madison Square Garden roof garden in 1906. "The Girl in the Red Velvet Swing" worked for Fox studio in Fort Lee. Nesbit's Fox films included *The Woman Who Gave* (1918) and *I Want to Forget* (1918).

Prior to becoming a star in Hollywood in the 1920s, Rudolph Valentino worked in the Fort Lee studios as an extra. His largest role was as a villain in *The Wonderful Chance* (Selznick Pictures Corporation, 1920). Valentino later teamed with another Fort Lee player, Nita Naldi, in the hit films *Blood and Sand* (1922), *A Sainted Devil* (1924), and *Cobra* (1925).

William Fox cornered the vamp market when he signed Valeska Suratt. She joined Virginia Pearson and the queen of vamps, Theda Bara, on the Fox lot in Fort Lee. The titles of Suratt's Fox films are indicative of her screen character—*Jealousy* (1916), *The Victim* (1916), and *The Slave* (1917). Her career ended with the demise of the vamp craze.

Josef Von Sternberg started his career as a film cutter for World Pictures in Fort Lee and was soon put in charge of all post-production at the studio. Von Sternberg ventured to Hollywood and directed for Paramount through the 1930s. He went to Germany to direct the classic *The Blue Angel* (1930) that made Marlene Dietrich a star, and later returned to Hollywood and directed Dietrich in a number of films at Paramount in the 1930s, including *Blonde Venus (1932)*.

Born Abigail Kane, theatrical actress Gail Kane starred with John Barrymore on Broadway and worked for Pathé and World. She made her film debut in 1913. Kane formed her own production company while in Fort Lee. Her films include *On Dangerous Ground* (1917). She died in 1966. Gail Kane's grandson donated her scrapbooks to the FLFC in 2002, and they are on permanent display at the Fort Lee Museum.

Maurice Tourneur was sent from his native France to Fort Lee in 1913 to work at the American Éclair studio on Linwood Avenue. The studio fire and other events led Tourneur to the World Film Corporation in Fort Lee. Tourneur's Fort Lee films include *Alias Jimmy Valentine* (1914), *The Wishing Ring* (1914), *Trilby* (1915), *A Girl's Folly* (1917), and *The Blue Bird* (1918).

Carlyle Blackwell is pictured on the lot at the World studio. He began his film career in 1910 at Vitagraph. He was a leading man and director for World Pictures in Fort Lee, where his films included *The Marriage Market* (1917), *Cabaret* (1918), and *Leap to Fame* (1918).

Most famous for her role as Glinda, the Good Witch of the North, in *The Wizard of Oz* (MGM, 1939), Billie Burke appeared in a number of films in Fort Lee. Two of these films were made for Famous Players–Lasky (Paramount): *Arms and the Girl* (1917) and *Good Gracious, Annabelle* (1920).

Paragon studio operator Gertrude Wagner Nestel is pictured here. She was one of many locals who gained employment at the studio.

A star of the westerns of John Ford, Harry Carey was born in the Bronx, New York, and made his first films for the Biograph Company under the direction of D. W. Griffith. His Fort Lee films for Biograph include *Friends* (1912), with fellow Biograph stock company members Lionel Barrymore and Mary Pickford, and *Heredity* (1912). One of the first gangster films, *The Musketeers of Pig Alley* (1912), features Carey with sisters Lillian and Dorothy Gish.

Ziegfeld Follies beauty Olive Thomas was hired by Selznick Pictures in Fort Lee, and starred in such films as *The Flapper* (1920). She was married to Mary Pickford's brother, Jack Pickford. On the verge of stardom, she died suddenly in Paris under mysterious circumstances. Olive's life was the subject of the 2003 documentary, *Olive Thomas: Everybody's Sweetheart*, directed by Andi Hicks and narrated by actress Rosanna Arquette for Timeline Films.

Mae Marsh's first lead role for Griffith was in *Man's Genesis* (1912). She also appeared in *The Birth of a Nation* (1915) and *Intolerance* (1916). Mae starred in Goldwyn's *Polly of the Circus* (1917), shot at the Goldwyn studio in Fort Lee, the first release of the newly formed Goldwyn Pictures Corporation.

Born in Canada in 1886, Florence Lawrence is generally considered the first movie star. Known as "the Biograph Girl," she appeared in over 270 films and made her first film at age 20. Her first film for Laemmle's IMP was *The Broken Oath* (1910), directed by her husband Harry Salter. In 1912, she and Salter created Victor Film Company. Lawrence committed suicide in Beverly Hills in 1938.

BLANCHE SWEET

Blanche Sweet began her film career with the Edison Company in 1909 at age 14. Sweet worked for a number of studios, including the Biograph Company, which nicknamed her "the Biograph Blonde." She left Biograph in 1914 and worked for Cecil B. DeMille in *The Warrens of Virginia* (1915). Sweet's roles for director D. W. Griffith include *The Battle* (1911), shot on Hammett's Hill in the Coytesville section of Fort Lee.

Director Albert Capellani was born in Paris in 1870. He began his career in cinema in 1905, when he started working for Pathé. Capellani made *L' Assommoir* (1909) for Pathé, one of the best early feature-length films. At the outbreak of World War I, he moved to the United States, where he directed for World Pictures in Fort Lee, and later founded Capellani Productions. His films include *Camille* (World, 1915).

In the early 1900s, American film audiences loved such child-women as Mary Pickford, Lillian Gish, and Marguerite Clark. Clark fit the part perfectly at four feet ten inches tall with dark brown hair and weighing only 90 pounds. She appeared with John Barrymore in the 1912 production of *The Affairs of Anatol*. In 1914, she signed with Lasky of Famous Players, and was ranked as the top actress of 1920.

Madge Kennedy planned to be an illustrator, but in 1912 found herself a Broadway star. She was signed in 1917 by the newly formed Goldwyn Company and worked in Goldwyn's Fort Lee studios. Her films include *Baby Mine* (1917), *Our Little Wife* (1918), and *The Kingdom of Youth* (1918). Kennedy made 21 films for Goldwyn. She later played the role of Aunt Martha in the television hit series *Leave it to Beaver* in 1957.

Born in Ireland, Owen Moore immigrated to the United States and entered the movies with Biograph Company in 1908. He appeared in many of Biograph's early productions shot in Fort Lee. Moore was Mary Pickford's leading man early in her career. They were wed in 1911 and appeared together in Biograph's *The Lonely Villa* (1909). Moore's last film was *A Star is Born* (1937). He died at age 52.

Elsie Ferguson, whose nickname was "the Aristocrat of the Screen," was a talented and much-married Broadway stage actress and silent film star. In 1916, Paramount-Artcraft's Adolph Zukor offered her a three-year contract. He paid her $5,000 per week for appearing in 18 pictures, the first of which was *Barbary Sheep* (1917), directed by Maurice Tourneur and shot at the Paragon studio on John Street.

The back lot of Paragon studio on John Street in Fort Lee was turned into an Algerian street set for Maurice Tourneur's *Barbary Sheep* (Paramount-Artcraft, 1917). *Barbary Sheep* star Elsie Ferguson appears on the trolley car on the set with her director Maurice Tourneur seated inside, as seen in this photograph.

Fort Lee residents (around 1917) pose on the same trolley car on the Paragon back lot used by Elsie Ferguson in the film *Barbary Sheep*.

One of the prime attractions of Fort Lee for early filmmakers was the natural beauty of the Palisades. The term "cliffhanger" found its origin on this rocky precipice, where serial queen Pearl White suffered her many perils, beginning in 1914. Featured in this photograph is a set up for an action sequence. Note the construction of a platform out of camera range to catch the actors. This photograph was donated to the FLFC from the collection of former Fort Lee resident George Symington, whose uncle was a cameraman for World Studios.

This photograph shows Fort Lee residents in line for a day's work at the Paragon studio on John Street for the film *Broadway Jones* (Cohan Feature Film Company-Artcraft, 1917). Everyone, including children, found extra work in Fort Lee. New York City children played hooky from school to take the ferry to Fort Lee where some earned as much as $75 a week for such work.

Pioneer African American filmmaker Oscar Micheaux worked in Fort Lee extensively from 1920 through 1948. *The Symbol of the Unconquered* (Micheaux Film Corporation, 1920), filmed on location in the Coytesville section of Fort Lee, had Micheaux directing on the same streets used by D. W. Griffith less than a decade earlier. Micheaux produced *The Exile* (Micheaux Film Corporation, 1931) at Metropolitan Studios in Fort Lee and promoted the film as the first all-black talking feature production. The FLFC, together with film historian Pearl Bowser, holds a yearly Micheaux film symposium at Fort Lee High School to educate students on the work of Micheaux in Fort Lee.

Bonded Film Storage opened in 1935 on the former Solax studio site on Lemoine Avenue. Bonded purchased the property from Consolidated, which purchased the property in 1931. Bonded operated at this site until 1965, when it was demolished to make way for an A&P supermarket. Bonded moved its storage facility to the former Republic studio/Consolidated site on the old Universal studio lot on Main Street in West Fort Lee. Hundreds of Fort Lee residents were employed in the film storage industry, as pictured here in these photographs.

Alice Joyce, born in Kansas City, Missouri, in 1890, was a telephone operator and fashion model prior to appearing in movies in 1910. She proved to be a charming leading lady in the early 1900s in the short films she made for Kalem Studios. She was known as "the Madonna of the Screen" and "the Kalem Girl." Joyce died in 1955.

Richard Barthelmess was born in New York City in 1895. D. W. Griffith starred him in his films *Broken Blossoms* (1919) and *Way Down East* (1920). Lillian Gish thought him the handsomest man who had ever been before the camera. He began his film career after amateur theater productions in *War Brides* (1916), playing opposite Alla Nazimova, which was a Selznick picture shot in the Ideal Studios.

Anna Nilsson
in
"Who's Guilty?" Series.

Anna Q. Nilsson was born in Sweden in 1888 and immigrated to America in 1910. Nilsson was hired for a role in the film *Molly Pitcher* (Kalem, 1911). She worked in many films for Famous Players, Paramount, Metro, Goldwyn, Mayflower, Warner Brothers, and First National. She died in 1974 and was the first Swedish actress to receive a star on the Hollywood Walk of Fame.

MGM executive Eddie Mannix, born in the Coytesville section of Fort Lee, started his career at the Palisades Amusement Park, working for Joseph and Nicholas Schenck who brought him to MGM. He returned to Fort Lee often and the local movie theater on Main Street and Center Avenue was renamed the Metro in honor of his studio MGM. Pictured here is Eddie Mannix at Palisades Amusement Park around 1923.

Joseph and Nicholas Schenck immigrated to New York City in 1893 and entered the amusement business in 1910 at Palisades Amusement Park, which they owned. The brothers both worked with theater operator Marcus Loew. Nicholas (right) took charge of the Loews empire in 1927. Joe signed Fatty Arbuckle to a contract in 1917 and was later the head of United Artists and 20th Century Fox.

Pictured here at a Joseph Schenck Productions party at Palisades Amusement Park during the 1920s are Joseph Schenck (wearing apron and seated in the center), composer Irving Berlin (fourth from the left), Constance Talmadge, Norma Talmadge, and Edgar Selwyn.

Born in California in 1883, Victor Fleming met film director Allan Dwan while working as a car mechanic, and Dwan took Fleming on as a camera assistant. Under Dwan's guidance, Fleming soon became a cinematographer working in Fort Lee on such productions as *Betty of Graystone* (Triangle-Fine Arts Studios, 1916). He died in 1949 at age 65.

Actors on the set of *The Better Wife* (Select Pictures, 1919) include Neil Hamilton, Barbara Tennant, and Norma Sulger. The film also starred Clara Kimball Young, who produced the movie at the local Oettel residence.

Raoul Walsh entered the movie industry as an actor and in 1914 became an assistant to D. W. Griffith. Walsh served Griffith as film editor, and assistant director and actor (playing the role of John Wilkes Booth) in *The Birth of a Nation* (D. W. Griffith Corporation, 1915). Walsh's Fort Lee period covers the time he worked as a director for William Fox.

Academy Award–winning actress and screenwriter Ruth Gordon was born in Quincy, Massachusetts, in 1896. She attended the American Academy of Dramatic Arts in New York City and appeared in silent films shot in Fort Lee, such as *Camille* (World, 1915). Gordon acted on the Broadway stage and later went to Hollywood. She won Best Supporting Actress for *Rosemary's Baby*, 1968, and died in 1985.

Silver screen character actor Adolphe Menjou was born in Pittsburgh in 1890. One of his many early, unbilled appearances is in a film directed by Allan Dwan, *The Habit of Happiness* (Triangle-Fine Arts, 1916) shot in Fort Lee. Menjou's Hollywood films include *The Front Page* (United Artists, 1931), *A Star is Born* (Selznick International Pictures, 1937), *One Hundred Men and a Girl* (Universal, 1937), the Stanley Kubrick film *Paths of Glory* (United Artists, 1957), and his final film *Pollyanna* (Walt Disney, 1960). Menjou died at age 73 in 1963.

Jean Arthur appeared in *Get That Venus* (Starmark Productions, 1933) shot at Metropolitan Sound Studios in Fort Lee. She is best known for her Frank Capra–directed classics, *Mr. Deeds Goes to Town* (Columbia Pictures, 1936), *You Can't Take It With You* (Columbia Pictures, 1938), and *Mr. Smith Goes to Washington* (Columbia Pictures, 1939). Born in upstate New York in 1900, Arthur died at the age of 90 in 1991.

Leading actor of the Yiddish stage, Maurice Schwartz was born in Russia in 1890 and immigrated to America in 1902. He founded the Yiddish Art Theater on Second Avenue in New York in 1926 and in that same year he directed and starred in his first film, *Broken Hearts* (Jaffe Art Films, 1926). Schwartz starred in *Uncle Moses* (Yiddish Talking Pictures Inc., 1932) shot at the Metropolitan studio in Fort Lee. He appeared in such Hollywood films as *Mission to Moscow* (Warner Brothers, 1943) and *Salome* (Columbia Pictures, 1953). Schwartz died at the age of 70 in 1960.

Academy Award–winning actress Norma Shearer was born in Canada in 1900. She started her film career in Fort Lee as an extra, and her first film role was in *The Flapper* (Selznick Pictures Corporation, 1920), starring Olive Thomas. Shearer married MGM production chief Irving Thalberg in 1927, and they were married until his death in 1936. Among her MGM films are *The Divorcee* (MGM, 1930), for which she won her Best Actress Oscar, and *The Women* (MGM, 1939). She retired in 1942 and died at the age of 82 in 1983.

Gene Gauntier, a writer and actress for the Kalem Company, claimed to be the first to recognize the value of Fort Lee as a motion picture location. Working with director Robert Vignola, Gauntier established Rambo's saloon as a base of operations in 1907. The Kalem unit filmed westerns and Civil War pictures all over Coytesville and Shadyside. The following year Gauntier moved to Biograph, where she informed the new director, D. W. Griffith, all about the scenic wonders of Fort Lee.

Ronald Colman was born in Richmond, Surrey, England, on February 9, 1891. He entered the British military during World War I and was severely injured in battle. Upon his return home, he entered the acting profession. Colman's first film appearance was in England in 1917. He came to New York in 1920; his first American film appearance was in *Handcuffs or Kisses?* (Selznick Pictures Corporation, 1921) shot in Fort Lee. Colman won an Academy Award for Best Actor for the film *A Double Life* (Universal, 1947). Among his best-remembered films is *A Tale of Two Cities* (MGM, 1935).

The ferry transportation system between 125th Street in Manhattan and the Edgewater Terminal was a key component of the growth of Fort Lee into a motion picture center. The ferry service combined with the then-new subway system allowed film companies located on 14th Street in Manhattan, such as Biograph, to send their crews and casts to Fort Lee for location work. This activity led to the building of a concentration of studios that gave Fort Lee the title of the first film town.

Director Frank Lloyd is seen here with a World War I doughboy on horseback on Linwood Avenue in front of Fox Studios. Lloyd acted in and directed films for companies such as Universal and Fox. His most important Fort Lee film was *Les Miserables* (1917). He went on to Hollywood where he directed films such as *Mutiny on the Bounty* (1935) and *The Last Command* (1955).

The Sen Jacq Film Print Company was built by Jules Brulatour in 1920 on property he owned adjacent to the Paragon studio. The Sen Jacq building, seen here in a photograph taken on September 15, 1923, is still active today as a motion picture warehouse. The FLFC stores its restored prints at this facility.

Jules Brulatour had a hand in financing most of the studios in Fort Lee and is arguably one of the most important figures in promoting the growth of the American movie industry. Brulatour was associated with many of Fort Lee's film companies, including the French-based Éclair Film Company, which opened a studio in Fort Lee in 1911.

The members of this local family were known to take pictures and pose on movie sets in Fort Lee. Note the actor playing the Prussian soldier on horseback riding up Tom Hunter Road.

Hoboken-born Éclair actress Dorothy Gibson was on the RMS *Titanic* when it sank on April 15, 1912. She survived the ordeal and returned to America. Six weeks later, the studio released *Escape From the Titanic*, the first movie filmed about the tragedy in which the actress portrayed herself, wearing the same outfit she wore during the actual sinking.

MARCONI WIRELESS TELEGRAPH COMPANY OF AMERICA.

27 WILLIAM STREET, (Lord's Court Building) NEW YORK.

Sent date ....

No. Prefix Code Words

Office of Origin

Service Instructions:

CHARGES TO PAY

Marconi Charge

Other Line Charge

Delivery Charge

Total

Time Sent By whom sent

To Dorothy Gibson Titanic

will do everything make you
completely happy love you madly

Julie

READ THE CONDITIONS PRINTED ON THE BACK OF THE FORM.

This Marconi Wireless telegraph was sent to actress Dorothy Gibson from Jules Brulatour who was waiting for her arrival in Fort Lee. Dorothy was having an affair with Brulatour at the time. Note that the telegraph was dispatched three days prior to the sinking of the Titanic.

Pete Cella's Hotel on Whiteman Street and Center Avenue was a gathering place for the Fort Lee movie companies. Many film events were held here, including the December 3, 1912, wedding of the film's first billed movie star, King Baggot, who worked for IMP and Universal.

Located on the edge of the Palisades off Hudson Terrace in Coytesville was the Villa Richard. The restaurant and its stone wall, which still stands, were the setting for many film shoots. The location was also the perfect spot for a radio station, WRNY, which became the first station to broadcast a television signal to 500 people in Manhattan on August 13, 1928. It later became Ben Marden's Riviera.

The Perils of Pauline (Pathé, 1914) was the most famous of all movie serials, starring the most famous of all serial queens, Pearl White. The action depicted in this movie poster reflected the nature of the serial and the promotional value of the cliffhanger. Notice the reference to "the 20th and Final Episode of *The Perils of Pauline.*" Eclectic Films Company was formed by Pathé to produce the film.

Four

MADE IN FORT LEE

From the time the first studios were established in the Fort Lee area, the movies were, by far, the region's largest employer. The 1918 *Industrial Directory of New Jersey* praised the borough's water, sewer, and transportation facilities, as well as its "ample supply of labor, both male and female," nearly all of whom were employed in the film industry. Of six "principle industries" listed in the directory, five were motion picture studios employing a total of 468 people. The only non-film business mentioned, a toy manufacturer, had 10 employees.

Although some of the stars and directors lived in the area, most of the workers were carpenters, painters, electricians, secretarial staff, and other hourly wage earners. The films they made were advertised, just like Hollywood's, with posters (usually 27 by 41 inches), lobby cards (11 by 14 inches) and colorful lantern slides all being used by theaters to promote their upcoming motion picture shows. While most of the fans may not have known where these films came from, Fort Lee's significance to the motion picture industry was well known in the trade.

After the First World War, many of these jobs were lost as the studios began to close down, but even then, film laboratories and warehouses continued to employ hundreds of local residents. As late as the 1970s, Consolidated Film Industries was still the central distribution point for most films shown in American theaters, as well as the advertising material that promoted them. Today the advertisements produced to sell these films remain the most compelling surviving records of Fort Lee's historic contribution to America's motion picture industry.

This lobby card features Arnold Daly and Anna Lehr in *My Own United States* (Metro Pictures, 1918). This film is based on the novel *The Man Without a Country*.

This glass movie slide promoted another Hope Hampton feature, *Stardust* (Hobart Henley Productions, 1922). The promotion of this film centered on the star of the picture, Hampton. The artwork for glass slides needed to be attractive, regardless of the quality of the film, as the goal was to fill seats in theaters.

American history provided the plot and the artwork for *Betsy Ross* (World Film Corporation, 1917). Alice Brady portrayed the colorful figure of the American Revolutionary, Betsy Ross. Also depicted in this glass slide is the colonial flag.

Tillie Wakes Up (World Pictures Corporation, 1917) starred Marie Dressler and Johnny Hines. Hines was a young yet skilled comedian who appeared in a number of Fort Lee films, including another World film, *A Girl's Folly* (World Pictures, 1917). Dressler had already starred in *Tillie's Punctured Romance* with Charlie Chaplin in 1914 in Los Angeles. Among her Fort Lee pictures was this popular comedy. The couple is portrayed to great comedic advantage in the glass slide pictured here.

He Did and He Didn't (Triangle-Keystone, 1916) was another successful movie in the "Fatty and Mabel" series. Filmed at the Triangle studio on Main Street and Linwood Avenue, this was one of Roscoe Arbuckle's most innovative films and took advantage of the screen charisma of the ever-popular Mabel Normand. As can be seen in this slide, Fatty and Mabel were clearly the marketing weapon used by their studio to sell this movie.

This production of *Les Miserables* (Fox Film Corporation, 1918) featured elaborate sets and high production values. Pictured on this glass slide is the star of the film, William Farnum. This Fox film, considered lost for decades, has recently turned up in Warsaw, Poland.

June Caprice normally appeared as the Fox studio version of Mary Pickford. The glass slide pictured here took advantage of a provocative and rarely seen side of this actress. Whether or not this film was "a dainty tale of thrills and adventure" would be left to the audience to decide.

Brother of director Raoul Walsh, George Walsh also worked for Fox Studios and was one of its most important stars. *This Is the Life* (Fox Film Corporation, 1917) was directed by Raoul Walsh and, as the glass slide shows, was sold as an action-adventure and a romance.

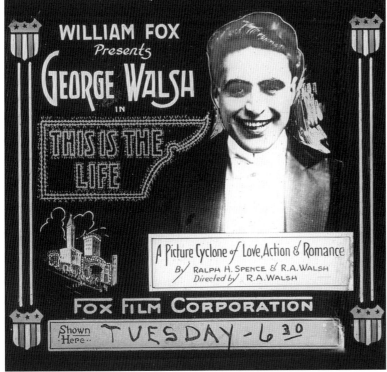

This Fox promotional display from 1916 featured the entire stable of Fox child stars, including Madge Evans. Child actresses were popular with audiences of this era and raked in money at the box office for the studios.

The Great Adventure (Pathé, 1918) was the final film directed in Fort Lee by Alice Guy Blaché, and starred Bessie Love. Bessie Love was the center of attention in the promotion of this film, as revealed by this glass slide. Glass slides would often highlight the actresses and depict them in attractive poses in order to lure customers to the box office.

Seen here is a *House of Hate* (Pathé, 1918) movie serial lobby card. Serial queen Pearl White appears with actor Antonio Moreno (in center, with his arm raised) and others in another chapter of this popular serial. Lobby cards promoted films with attractive images and photographs.

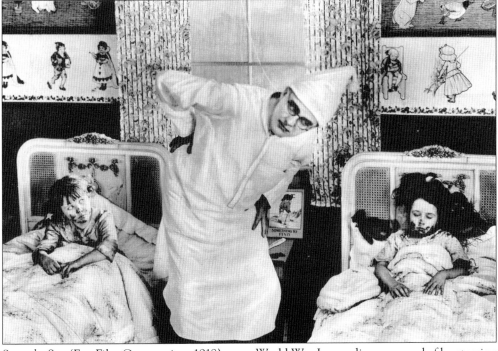

Swat the Spy (Fox Film Corporation, 1918) was a World War I comedic propaganda film starring Fox's box office child stars Jane and Katherine Lee. This lobby card featured the sisters described as "two imps" who strafed the Kaiser's crew.

Fox vamp Theda Bara was depicted in lobby cards, glass slides, and posters as a sex symbol in an era when sex was a forbidden topic in public discourse. *Gold and the Woman* (Fox Film Corporation, 1916) was directed by James Vincent. This glass slide depicted Bara in a more subdued appearance as the daughter of a Mexican aristocrat caught in the midst of the Mexican Revolution.

The Danger Game (Goldwyn Pictures Corporation, 1918) featured actress Madge Kennedy. Kennedy was a popular silent film actress whose career lasted for decades. This lobby card captured Kennedy in a scene that does not indicate exactly where the danger is coming from, but leaves the moviegoer guessing.

This lobby card depicts screen heartthrob Rudolph Valentino in a rare role as a villain in the film *The Wonderful Chance* (Selznick Pictures, 1920). Valentino, pictured here with gun in hand as he is strangled by hero Eugene O'Brien, would later go on to more traditional romantic fare. Action sold at the box office and was a source of material for studio marketing executives.

War Brides (Selznick Pictures, 1916) featured Russian born actress Alla Nazimova in her first movie. This picture was made by Herbert Brenon at the Ideal Studios and released by Selznick Pictures. This advertisement not only featured the stars, but also director Brenon.

Brennan of the Moor (Solax, 1913) is depicted in this poster as a mysterious masked man on horseback, a kind of Irish Robin Hood. The poster pictured here left nothing to the imagination, overtly showing how Brennan of the Moor is worshipped by the poor.

World Studios comedian Johnny Hines is pictured in this lobby card from *The Cub* (World Pictures Corporation, 1915), a film directed by Maurice Tourneur. If this lobby card is to be believed, Hines not only won the girl, but also many of her gun-toting relatives.

The Little Giant (Universal, 1925) was shot at the Universal studio on Main Street. Glenn Hunter is featured as the lead and appeared with attractive costar Edna Murphy in the lobby card pictured here. This was the final film Universal produced in Fort Lee.

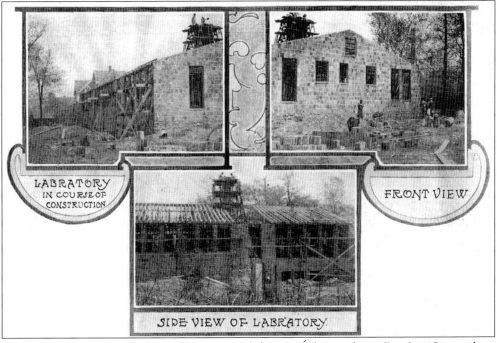

The Billboard magazine of July 8, 1911, promoted the new Éclair studio in Fort Lee. Pictured are photographs of the studio and film laboratory under construction. Studios took out advertisements in industry magazines that promoted their operations and helped to create business.

Pictured here at the March 13, 2004, unveiling of an FLFC historic marker on the original site of Solax studio on Lemoine Avenue are, from left to right, former FLFC chairman Lou Azzollini, FLFC member Rutgers University professor Richard Koszarski, Alice Guy Blaché biographer Alison McMahan, FLFC executive director Tom Meyers, and FLFC liaison councilman Armand Pohan. This marker is the first and only one in the world dedicated to the first woman of the cinema, Alice Guy Blaché.

Alice Guy Blaché's great-granddaughter, Nicki Sanchez, attended a book signing for *Alice Guy Blaché: Lost Visionary of the Cinema* by Alison McMahan at Borders Books in Fort Lee on March 13, 2004. McMahan and Sanchez attended the unveiling of the FLFC sign dedicated to Alice Guy Blaché earlier that day.

Five

FORT LEE TODAY

"Fort Lee Today" takes us from 1948 (the last film production in a Fort Lee studio) to the present. Fort Lee still serves as a location for filmmakers. To film key scenes for their film noir classic, *Kiss of Death* (20th century Fox, 1947), 20th Century Fox returned to Fort Lee. Fox shot exteriors and interiors at the Academy of the Holy Angels, which was situated across the street from Fox's first studio on Main Street and Linwood Avenue.

The George Washington Bridge, which opened in 1931, brought filmmakers to Fort Lee and appears in films, such as *The House on 92nd Street* (20th Century Fox, 1945), *Force of Evil* (Enterprise Productions, Inc., 1948), Alfred Hitchcock's *The Wrong Man* (Warner Brothers, 1956), and *Cop Land* (Miramax, 1997).

The most interesting film shot in Fort Lee in the modern era was *Goodfellas* (Warner Brothers, 1990). Director Martin Scorsese, who is a leading film scholar, knows the history of film in Fort Lee and shot key scenes of this film blocks away from locations used by D. W. Griffith in the first classic gangster film, *The Musketeers of Pig Alley* (Biograph, 1912). More recently, the tradition of gangster films lives on through the HBO series *The Sopranos*, which has used Fort Lee as a location numerous times over the life of the series. Directors, companies, and organizations, like the FLFC, have tried to keep up Fort Lee's role as a burgeoning film town.

The FLFC was organized by the Borough of Fort Lee in 2000. Its projects include the creation of a twice-a-year film retrospective series under the banner of "Cliffhanger." The Cliffhanger 2003 Spring Film Festival centered on the first large-scale public viewing of the only existing print of the first film version of Frankenstein. *Frankenstein* (Edison Company, 1910) was screened at the Landmark Loews in Jersey City to a sellout audience. This festival led to the film's owner, Al Detlaff, sending the FLFC the only existing print of the first American film version of Robin Hood, *Robin Hood* (American Éclair, 1912), which was restored by the FLFC in 2006.

The FLFC held a Roscoe "Fatty" Arbuckle retrospective, "Fatty In Fort Lee" in April 2005. Pictured at the April 10, 2005, symposium at the Fort Lee Historic Park Theater are, from left to right, *Forgotten Films of Roscoe Arbuckle* (Laughsmith Entertainment Inc., 2005) executive producer Bruce Lawton, film historian Steve Massa, *Forgotten Films of Roscoe Arbuckle* director and executive producer Paul E. Gierucki, executive producer Brittany Valente, and symposium moderator Richard Koszarski.

The FLFC's Cliffhanger 2006 Spring Film Festival was a "Salute to Fox Studios." Pictured here is festival guest Academy Award–winning actress Celeste Holm and moderator Christina Kotlar, managing editor of the *Film Festival Reporter*. Prior to the symposium, the FLFC screened *All About Eve* (20th Century-Fox, 1950), starring Holm. The FLFC presented Holm with the 2006 FLFC Barrymore Award for her contributions as an actress and one of the founders of the New Jersey Motion Picture and Television Commission.

The FLFC actively seeks film production shoots in Fort Lee. Pictured here in December 2004 from left to right are FLFC executive director Tom Meyers, NBC *Late Night*'s Conan O'Brien, FLFC former chair Lou Azzollini, and FLFC volunteer Scott Manginelli in Fort Lee during a *Late Night With Conan O'Brien* shoot.

New Jersey–born comedian Lou Costello has been honored by the FLFC with annual film festivals, which have been attended by his daughter Chris Costello. Here during a 2002 festival, Chris Costello poses at the statue of her dad in Paterson with, from left to right, unidentified, Paterson police chief Larry Spagnola, Lou Azzollini of the FLFC, Paterson mayor Jose "Joey" Torres, Costello, Tom Meyers of the FLFC, boxing promoter Lou Duva, and Lou Cucinello. Duva and Cucinello were the driving force behind the building of the statue in Lou Costello's hometown.

Documentary filmmaker Andi Hicks of the Mary Pickford Institute of Los Angeles appeared at a FLFC screening of her documentary *Olive Thomas: Everybody's Sweetheart* (Timeline Films, 2004) at the Fort Lee Historic Park in May 2005. Olive Thomas was a star with Selznick Pictures of Fort Lee. Pictured here with Hicks is FLFC member and film historian Richard Koszarski.

The FLFC inaugurated the annual Jersey Filmmakers of Tomorrow Film Festival for high school students in May 2005 with a kickoff press conference at Fort Lee High School. Attending the press conference from left to right are actor Dominick Chianese of *The Sopranos*, Fort Lee borough administrator Peggy Thomas, Bergen County executive and festival cosponsor Dennis McNerney, FLFC executive director Tom Meyers, and liaison councilman Armand Pohan.

Pictured here during a break in the 2004 shoot for *The Thing About My Folks* (Picturehouse, 2005) are actor Peter Falk, FLFC executive director Tom Meyers, actor and writer Paul Reiser, and FLFC secretary Donna Brennan. The FLFC was successful in bringing this production to Fort Lee.

The Thing About My Folks crew is pictured at work on location in Fort Lee around 2004. This shoot involved streets in the Coytesville section of Fort Lee, as well as the Palisades Interstate Park.

Associate members of the FLFC include Eric Nelsen of the Palisades Interstate Park Commission and legendary broadcasting icon Joe Franklin seen here at the Cliffhanger 2000 Fall Film Festival "Horror on the Palisades" salute to silent horror films at the Fort Lee Historic Park.

The Cliffhanger festival is held in the spring and fall each year and focuses on various themes of filmmaking. Guest stars at the "Salute to Universal Studios and Abbott and Costello" from left to right are Gil Palmer as Bud, "Uncle Floyd" Vivino, veteran funnyman Charlie Callas, and Lou Sciarra as Lou.

Featured in this picture are Richard Koszarski and Nelson Page outside the historic Rambo's saloon during a January 2004 Fort Lee *Today* shoot. This was the same location used by filmmakers and actors such as D. W. Griffith, Lionel Barrymore, Florence Lawrence, and Milton Berle. Sports figures, such as Babe Ruth and Max Schmelling, also patronized this saloon.

Jersey Filmmakers of Tomorrow Film Festival finalists are pictured with 2005 FLFC Barrymore Award honoree and Academy Award–winning film editor Thelma Schoonmaker during the November 2005 FLFC awards dinner. The FLFC named the award after the actor John Barrymore who made his stage debut in Fort Lee at the age of 18 during a fire department fund-raiser staged by his father Maurice Barrymore.

Theda Bara gets her way in Fort Lee, as a sign designating the corner of Main Street and Linwood Avenue as Theda Bara Way is unveiled. Pictured here during the May 2006 ceremony are, from left to right, FLFC former chair Lou Azzollini, FLFC member Richard Koszarski, FLFC liaison councilman Armand Pohan, filmmakers Denise Morse, Andi Hicks, Hugh Munro Neely, FLFC executive director Tom Meyers, volunteers Scott Manginelli, Kevin Ceragno, and Fort Lee poet laureate August Klenizahler.

FLFC members Nelson Page, Tom Meyers, and Richard Koszarski pose with Cliffhanger 2005 Fall Film Festival "View From the Bridge" guest actress and teacher Julie Garfield. Garfield, the daughter of actor John Garfield, spoke before a screening of her father's classic film *Force of Evil* (1948). The film featured the George Washington Bridge to great effect as a location. She also appeared in *Goodfellas* (Warner Brothers, 1990), which was partially shot in Fort Lee.

Director Martin Scorsese is one of the leaders of the American film preservation movement and a great film historian. Pictured here with Scorsese is Lake Placid Film Festival official Kathleen Carroll and FLFC chairman Nelson Page, who also serves as the Lake Placid Film Festival director.

Pictured here is the 2003 FLFC Barrymore Award winner actress Lorraine Bracco (right) with her *The Sopranos* costar Vincent Curatola and Lou Costello's daughter Chris at the FLFC awards dinner. Bracco not only appeared in an episode of *The Sopranos* shot in Fort Lee, she was also featured in *Goodfellas* in scenes filmed in Fort Lee.

Actor Peter Riegert is pictured here receiving the 2004 FLFC Barrymore Award from FLFC chairman Nelson Page. Riegert shot part of his film *King of the Corner* (2004) in Fort Lee.

The Pordenone Silent Film Festival in Italy honored Fort Lee in October 2004 on the centennial of the borough. Pictured here from left to right are FLFC executive director Tom Meyers, Pordenone festival director Livio Jacob, and FLFC member Richard Koszarski, after a screening of Fort Lee films at the theater in Sacile. Koszarski's book *Fort Lee: The Film Town* was featured at this festival.

Film historian and Oscar Micheaux scholar Pearl Bowser appears in Fort Lee yearly for a Micheaux symposium, staged at Fort Lee High School jointly by the FLFC and Fort Lee High School principal Jay Berman. Bowser is pictured here during a February 2005 lecture prior to a screening of a Micheaux film shot in Fort Lee.

Pictured here is actor and director Tim Reid interviewing Oscar Micheaux scholar Pearl Bowser in the Fort Lee Museum in February 2004 for an episode of the *American Legacy* television program. This episode highlighted pioneer African American filmmaker Oscar Micheaux's work in Fort Lee from 1920–1948.

The FLFC sponsors a Movies and Music Under the Stars program for 12 weeks each summer. Pictured here is the audience at Constitution Park enjoying a film on a summer night. Constitution Park is the former home to numerous studios, including Éclair.

The FLFC received the 2006 Bergen County Historic Preservation Leadership Award for the preservation of the film, *Robin Hood*. Pictured above from left to right are volunteer Kevin Ceragno, FLFC former chairman Lou Azzollini, FLFC executive director Tom Meyers, Bergen County Parks director Frank DeBari, FLFC vice chair Kay Nest, New Jersey assemblywoman Valerie Vaineri-Huttle, Joan Voss, and Bergen County Cultural and Heritage Affairs director Carol Messer.

Director Martin Scorsese's epic gangster film *Goodfellas* (Warner Brothers, 1990) was partially shot in Fort Lee. This movie carried on the tradition of filmmaking in Fort Lee that goes back to the days of D. W. Griffith's *The Musketeers of Pig Alley* (Biograph, 1912).

New Jersey native Frank Sinatra had roots not only in his hometown of Hoboken, but in nearby Fort Lee, where he performed at the Riviera Nightclub and visited his parents' home on Abbott Boulevard. Pictured here are newlyweds Frank Sinatra and Mia Farrow, around 1967, outside Sinatra's parents' house in Fort Lee. Sinatra also filmed *Contract on Cherry Street* (1977) in the Fort Lee area.

ACROSS AMERICA, PEOPLE ARE DISCOVERING
SOMETHING WONDERFUL. *THEIR HERITAGE.*

Arcadia Publishing is the leading local history publisher in the United States. With more than 3,000 titles in print and hundreds of new titles released every year, Arcadia has extensive specialized experience chronicling the history of communities and celebrating America's hidden stories, bringing to life the people, places, and events from the past. To discover the history of other communities across the nation, please visit:

www.arcadiapublishing.com

Customized search tools allow you to find regional history books about the town where you grew up, the cities where your friends and family live, the town where your parents met, or even that retirement spot you've been dreaming about.

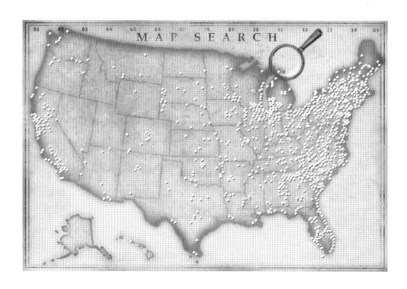